Self-Esteem

Gaining More Mental Control May Be Accomplished Through Working On One's Social Skills As Well As One's Emotional Intelligence

(Conquer Anxiety, Get Over Shyness, Improve Your People Skills And Boost Your Self-confidence)

Cyril Leach

TABLE OF CONTENT

Introduction 1

Who You Should Comprise Your Inner Circle With 12

Increase Your Level Of Self-Confidence By Working On Your Sense Of Self-Worth. 44

Take The Time To Listen To Your Own Ideas. 52

Get What You Can Out Of Your Relationships. 57

Putting Your Objectives Down In Writing On Paper 70

Take The Time To Listen To Your Own Ideas. 78

Superior Capabilities In The Field Of Entrepreneurship 87

Instruments That Can Help A Person Become More Self-Aware 93

Increasing One's Level Of Self-Assurance Is Associated With An Increase In Overall Happiness. 105

Smart Methods For Maintaining Your Motivation 114

What The Opinions Of Other People Are 131

Conclusion 150

Introduction

There is a very reasonable explanation for why issues with one's self-esteem are becoming more prevalent in today's society. It should come as no surprise that some individuals have the feeling that they don't live up to the standards that society expects of them, given the rising rates of divorce and the increased pressure placed on people to attain their goals. It is difficult to be flawless, and yet we are constantly exposed to examples of individuals who seem to be picture perfect on the covers of magazines and on our television screens. We are also exposed to commercials for all of the items that may assist us in living up to those ideals; yet, the majority of these claims are just hype.

How do you get beyond such a pessimistic outlook on life after you've recognised that there's something wrong with the way you look at yourself? That is the purpose of the experiment we are doing. We are certain that the methods that we have developed for you to use inside these pages of this book will assist you in moving beyond the stage of feeling horrible about who you are. They will also help you build up your self-confidence so that you may confront the world that you live in with optimism and a positive attitude.

The techniques described in this book have been shown to be effective, and it will be useful to attempt each one in turn since each of them contributes to your levels of self-assurance, although the application of a single technique may not be sufficient on its own. Therefore, read through the whole book. After you've given the workouts we provide a go, step back and take a fresh look at who you are. You will be aware of your own worth, and you won't want the approval of others to be satisfied with who you are. This is significant because individuals who struggle with low self-esteem are often looking for approval from other people. You need to quit doing that right now because even if other people validate you, it won't make much of a difference in how you feel about yourself even if you do it. At the end of the day, the only opinion that matters is the one you have to live with since it is the only one you have control over.

You will learn how to be successful and feel good about yourself by consciously deciding not to seek validation from other people, which is one of the skills that we will teach you. Instead, the tasks that are included in this experiment are ones that only need the permission of one person: yourself. Figure out how to feel good about the encounters you have with other people. Learn to take pleasure in being yourself. When you finally understand it, you will never again feel that you are lacking in any way, since that is what life is all about.

You may begin overcoming low self-esteem and become the person you want for yourself by following these seven suggestions.

Put Yourself in the Company of Positive Individuals.

A dislike for powerful people in one's life is frequently the first step on the path to developing low self-esteem. For instance, if you were often told that you don't measure up or if you were criticised for everything that you did, this might prevent you from maturing into a brave adult with a good mental image of yourself. To assist you in developing your bravery, you should make an effort to surround yourself with good, dependable people who acknowledge and reinforce your positive characteristics, such as your commitments, and who really boost you. This will aid you.

Learn Even More About Yourself, and Make Yourself Your Best Friend by Learning More About Yourself

You are important and have the right to enjoy who you are, regardless of the ways in which you vary from others. Spend time by yourself and make time to get to know yourself better. This will help you to determine whether or not you are one of a kind, distinctive, and respectable, which will enable you to acquire a higher value for yourself. Consequently, spend time alone and make time for getting to know yourself better. You might also try writing a list of your successes and traits as a way to assist yourself in remembering who you are. After you have completed the list, you can go back to it whenever you need a boost in self-esteem and want to feel better about yourself.

This is also an excellent moment to identify any negative thoughts that you have about yourself and confront them head-on.

Recognise the Areas in Which You Need to Make Changes

We all have problems, but if you do not see and confess the areas in which you need to make changes, it might trap you in a cycle of low self-esteem that will only become worse the more you try to run away from it. If you do not recognise and admit the areas in which you need to make changes, it could be a trap for you. Instead, cultivate awareness and recognition of the areas in which you need change, and then put in the effort to better those areas. You may even enlist the assistance of a close friend or a member of your family.

You should also be mindful of the times when you are too critical of yourself and then remind yourself that the criticisms you have of yourself are not based in reality. This will assist you in maintaining a healthy distance from the unpleasant emotions that may lead to negative self-talk.

Make an effort to avoid comparing yourself to other people.

Psychotherapists warn that drawing such links only leads to a negative mental self-view, which in turn may lead to low self-esteem, tension, and uneasiness, all of which can be detrimental to one's professional and personal life, as well as one's physical and mental health.

Affirmations positive should be repeated.

In a similar vein, just as one might accept negative affirmations such as "you are an idiot," one can also choose to disbelieve them. Therefore, it is recommended by therapists that you repeat positive affirmations that you need to accept about yourself on a regular basis in order to assist you in making a seamless transition back to a time when you suffered from low self-esteem. In point of fact, research have shown that positive affirmations may even aid in lessening the side effects of sorrow and other negative emotions.

Take care of yourself first.

Simple habits like washing your face, combing your hair, wearing clean clothes, maintaining a healthy diet, and regularly engaging in physical activity will help you have a positive self-image.

In addition, a plethora of studies have shown that elevating the quality of your living place to one that is enticing, flawless, and comfy will assist enhance your mood.

Donate Your Time

Giving to others, donating your time, and assisting those who are less fortunate not only diverts your attention away from your own problems but also makes you feel good about yourself since you are making a positive difference in the lives of other people. According to research, increasing the number of things in your life that you can look back on with satisfaction and feel proud of has a positive effect on your self-worth, which in turn makes you feel better about yourself.

Last but not least, people who have a healthy respect for themselves are open to growth and more meaningful experiences. This indicates that they do not rely on external fortifications, such as position or pay, for their sense of self-worth. As a result, they are able to enjoy a higher level of fulfilment and take pleasure in the journey that is life. Be mindful of the people you let into your life as well as the circumstances that you let determine how much value you place on yourself. You should also make an effort to take care of yourself by engaging in healthy behaviours, including as going to the gym and eating well, so that you can keep your body and mind in good shape.

Who You Should Comprise Your Inner Circle With

I sat down with my group of friends around a year and a half ago; I hadn't seen them in a very long time. I usually made it a point to try and listen to them as much as possible rather to ramble on about what I was interested in, even if there were moments when I could talk for England.

While I was having a few drinks, I remained attentive to what they were saying. They were discussing their careers as well as the mortgages that they had.

They were discussing their romantic relationships, upcoming nuptials, and expectancies at the time. Even though I was happy for them, I couldn't help but feel that it would be inappropriate to speak about the things that attracted me, such as reading, self-improvement, my books, coaching, or ideas, even if I was thrilled that they were successful.

I didn't have to wait long after that until I saw another bunch of my buddies. They had been some of my closest friends throughout my childhood, and we'd had many memorable experiences together throughout that period. I had the idea of once again asking them about them, and despite the fact that they were interested in my books, I was still under the impression that I couldn't have an interesting discussion with them.

It seemed to me, just like it had in the other group, that discussing the books I'd read, the things I wanted to do in life, and the many other pursuits I'd taken an interest in wouldn't make for an appropriate discourse.

One day, I was having a discussion with a person who was really close to me. The individual inquired about the amount of time and money I put into personal growth, as well as the level of risk associated with doing so. Because of this, I was left feeling dejected and, to some extent, furious. Because I had made the decision to no longer discuss my personal development interests with that particular individual, I chose to maintain my silence.

Of course, I continued to communicate with them, but our conversations did not revolve on those topics.

After that, I began going to personal development and coaching groups as well as Toastmasters. It was really simple for me to strike up conversations with the locals there. They could listen to me, and I could listen to them at the same time. I was able to build some wonderful connections, and while I was in their company, I felt like I was really living. The same was true of my coaches and mentors; we were able to have open conversations about my goals and the next steps I should take to achieve them.

You should be able to make out stuff happening up there.

When I was among some individuals, I felt as if my life force and vitality were being stifled, but when I was around others who shared my values, I felt fantastic. It is essential to stress that there is nothing wrong with the groups of friends and someone close to me that I described; it is simply that they do not have the same vision, and their energies and perspectives on life are different from one another.

It has been my good fortune to have typically been able to avoid becoming friends with negative individuals, but as I continue to develop myself, I have encountered situations in which others just do not understand me.

The thing that I started to understand, and the thing that I began to observe, was that whenever I surrounded myself with individuals who didn't grasp it, I began to question my own abilities. I don't know when exactly I picked up the wisdom to keep negative individuals out of my life, but I do know that I did it very early on.

When I am in settings and personal development groups with other individuals who are like me, I begin to feel wonderful.

The takeaway here is that you should be selective about the places and people with whom you choose to spend your time. When it comes to family members and, more often than not, close friends, it may not be simple to just ignore them or eliminate them from your life. You might instead chat about topics that you two have in common.

Avoid getting involved in talks in which you and the other person can disagree, since this will only serve to aggravate both of you. Find some helpful advisors, coaches, and online communities where individuals share your interests. This will lift you up and give you the opportunity to be the true version of yourself. It is possible to have the sensation that there is a cage around you when you limit yourself from being honest, which may have a very damaging effect on your sense of self-worth.

Take action:

This is something that I did over the last year that had a significant impact on my life. It is not necessary that it be a costly endeavour. Visit a website like MeetUp and browse for activities that interest you, such as fitness, nutrition, personal development, or singing. You may also look for others who share your interests. The next step is to locate groupings of those items. Join one and go to the meetings. If you think this is a significant matter, consider it in the following terms:

a) List your interests; b) Search on MeetUp (or another website); c) Look at groups and list them; d) Ask information if required; e) Say you will attend; e) Attend - only one event; e) Then attend two more events.

I believe that testing out new groupings using the rule of three is a smart idea. This is something that my Toastmasters speaking group and I performed together. The first time I went, I didn't know anybody there, and my mind was telling me that I didn't belong there. Then I stayed true to my word and went all the way to three. Before I knew it, I was giving many talks, meeting new friends, and really adoring myself in this environment. My new role includes offering coaching for public speaking in addition to mentoring others. If I had quit up after the first two tries, none of this would have transpired.

Summary and Analysis of Chapter 9

This short book was intended to assist you in enhancing your sense of self-worth in a straightforward, seven-step process. You now have a better understanding of what self-esteem is, how it may grow in either a good or bad direction, and the influence it has on your life. After that, we went through the seven stages in further depth to help you build your self-esteem. In addition, we wrapped off each chapter with a plan of action for putting that specific step into practise, as well as some exercises to help you get a better grasp on the information that was presented.

We have the utmost faith that if you merely put in the effort required to follow these seven steps, you will see a significant improvement in the quality of your life. The following are, once again, the 7 steps:

1. Confronting the Problems That Come From Having a Low Self-Esteem. 2. Participating in Psychotherapy or Counselling.

3. The Influence of Having a Positive Mental Attitude

4. Transforming Defeat into Victory in the Long Run

5. Persistent efforts towards one's own personal development

6. Refrain from Strive for Perfection

7. Make a Festive Occasion Out of Celebrating Your Own Self-Esteem

Be trustworthy and honest, and proceed with these instructions. Soon, you will have such a positive opinion of yourself that you will question when and why you ever felt the need to work on boosting your self-esteem in the first place. Just Get It Done!

Negative thoughts and feelings of depression

When you are sad, you have a propensity to think negatively, which gets us back to the first argument, which is that negative thinking is associated with depression. It is simply because of the unfavourable method in which your brain is working at that particular instant. You are having trouble absorbing the chemicals that make you joyful, and since your body is unable to take them in, you are not seeing any positive changes in your behaviour. If you are not experiencing any pleasure from what you are doing, then there is no use in making an effort to alter what you are doing. You have the perception that everything is worthless, and since you have this perception, it is difficult for you to work up the motivation to make changes. Again, we see that circle repeating itself; negativity begets other instances of negativity.

Because you are unable to genuinely alter your attitude, you have the persistent sensation that your depression is becoming justified, or even becoming worse in certain cases. This is due to the fact that you are unable to change your mindset. You are unable to move on from the negative ideas because they are both self-defeating and self-perpetuating. Despite the fact that you despise the thoughts in their current form, you believe they are legitimate, and this justification causes you to detest yourself more deeply than you did before. You start to talk to yourself in negative ways, telling yourself that you are imperfect, worthless, or unworthy of respect, success, or pleasure. You begin to describe yourself as a failure. These ideas keep you down, which worsens your depression and makes it more difficult for you to break the pattern and move on with your life.

Nevertheless, this is something that can be altered; you have the ability to rid yourself of negative thinking and ease some of the symptoms of depression. You may not be able to quickly alter the chemical makeup of your brain in order to make things more enjoyable for you, but at the very least, you will be able to see the benefit of using positive language and engaging in good behaviour. You are about to see firsthand how a positive attitude may alter the outcomes.

The Effects That Thinking Negatively Has On Your Life

Do you have faith that things will be better in the future than they are right now? Are you able to affirm with absolute certainty that you feel tomorrow will be an improvement over today? This question may be responded to with a simple "Yes," "No," or "Maybe." Whether you want to believe it or not, your response right now will determine how your future unfolds. The method in which we think gives rise to the lives that we lead.

A query is as follows: Why do we let ourselves get worked up over everything? Why do we go into every scenario assuming the worst possible outcome? The reason for this is because we really care. The idea that you are now one step closer to ridding your mind of pessimistic and negative thoughts was the impetus behind your decision to purchase this book. Now, let's give it a go.

The habitual processing of negative thoughts gives rise to negativity. This line of thought is prompted by negative events in the past the vast majority of the time. This might be in the shape of a previous experience of failure, rejection, being taken for granted, prejudice, and so on and so forth. If a person, for instance, has been through a significant number of setbacks in their life at various points in the past, they will gradually adopt a new way of thinking. They might start thinking that achieving their goals is impossible, which is a dangerous belief to have. They could also come to the conclusion that being successful in life is unattainable rather quickly. They will develop a pessimistic outlook, which they will then apply to each and every circumstance. They come across throughout the course of their existence. In a nutshell, they transform into a pessimist.

A pessimist is someone whose mind is always preoccupied with negative ideas, which are mirrored in their feelings and emotions, and which, as a result, give off an attitude that is negative. This cycle never ends, and it causes them to lose any sense of self in the process. As individuals go through life, it is only normal for them to focus more on the unfavourable aspects of situations.

Pessimists, often known as those who think negatively, have a consistent pattern of behaviour and thought. This tendency is supported by an ongoing stream of negative ideas. There are four primary categories of pessimistic thinking that make up these patterns.

The need to have everything just so is the root of the "all-or-nothing" way of thinking. It is essential that perfection be attained; anything less than that is an outright failure. One such way of thinking is one that rejects everything and everything that is good. It immediately casts off any glimmer of optimism and leaps to the conclusion that everything in life will ultimately result in dissatisfaction. Another kind of negative self-labeling is one in which shortcomings are celebrated and openly acknowledged. This kind of thought believes that a person is not deserving of affection and appreciation. The last of the four categories of negative thinking is known as catastrophizing. It accentuates the negative aspects of every and every circumstance and focuses on the most dire outcomes possible.

Having a belief system that is restrictive prevents us from living the life that we really want. You are making matters worse for yourself by digging deeper into a hole that you previously hoped you weren't in. Have you been living in a consistent pattern of unfavourable thinking and behaviour? Are you able to acknowledge that it has had a significant impact on your life?

Imagine now how adopting a more optimistic outlook may transform your life. It is an extremely potent secret that has been handed down from generation to generation. It is just necessary for us to learn how to implement it into our day-to-day lives.

Altering Emotions in Response to Their Surroundings

Your surroundings have a significant bearing on your state of mind, in particular if you are a compassionate person. You take on the mood around you and feed off of it; if the mood is tight and anxious, you are certain to absorb some of that anxiety as well. You draw on and feed off of the atmosphere around you. If you have the impression that the surrounding environment is hazardous, you will have environmental anxiety. Being in a setting where other people are also depressed and miserable can bring out your own feelings of melancholy.

Because of this, it is of the utmost need to exercise caution over the kind of people with whom you surround yourself. If you want to retain a joyful attitude, you need to surround yourself with positive people who are appreciative of you and nice to you. You need to be in an atmosphere that is favourable to just that—quiet and relaxation—if you want to be peaceful and relaxed, as well as feel confident in your surroundings. The way in which other people act will provide your body with cues as to how it should conduct itself. You will feel more at ease when the mannerisms of others around you indicate that there is nothing to be concerned about. You will experience an increase in your level of energy if individuals around you seem to be experiencing the same level of energy.

In the end, as human beings, we are social animals by the very essence of our species. When we communicate, we take cues from the world around us. We are able to detect the feelings of our friends and family members in the air, in our surroundings, and these feelings have a significant influence on us.

Stop what you're doing and take a glance about you if you want to alter the feelings you're experiencing. Is it a stringent policy? Is it abrasive and distressing to you? Do you sense that you are cherished and protected? If you are unable to say that you are content and at ease in the relationship you are currently in, it is time to think about how you might remove yourself from the unhealthy atmosphere.

Harmful surroundings can only produce more harmful outcomes. The sole result of being in a negative atmosphere is more negativity. It is OK to rid your life of the negativity and poison that it contains, regardless of how familiar or comfortable the situation may seem. Should you choose to do so, your mental health will be grateful to you for it.

Additionally, if you want to influence your mood to be happier and more energised, surrounding yourself with positive energy is something you should do. Gather a close circle of supportive people around you. Put on some music that has a lot of energy and puts you in the mood to move about. If the atmosphere around you is one that encourages you to relax and have fun, there is a far better chance that you will do so.

In the end, you will have to acknowledge the fact that your feelings are influenced by the surrounding environment. Your feelings will almost always be a reflection of the people and things that you surround yourself with, and it's perfectly OK for this to happen. Nevertheless, if you are surrounded by unhealthy influences, you owe it to yourself and the people you care about to make changes. Even if they are members of your own family, you do not have any need to put up with poisonous people. You are perfectly within your rights to terminate a connection with someone, regardless of whether it is familial, romantic, or platonic, if you believe that the environment you are in has to be abandoned because it is poisonous.

Keep in mind that just as it is possible to cultivate a plant almost everywhere, it is conceivable that you will survive almost anyplace. You will be able to make it through even if you are surrounded by poison. However, you will not be successful. In the same way that certain plants may survive outside of their natural environments but do not flourish there, you can make it through life alive but you will not be the best that you can be. Discovering the community to which you are most suited is the most effective strategy for becoming the greatest version of yourself. It is possible to find it if one is willing to put in the effort, but it is out there someplace.

Increasing your productivity by working on projects that are outside of your comfort zone

Your self-assurance has been chipped at by life's experiences over the years. It did not take place in an instant, and you should not expect to see immediate consequences that will assist you in regaining control of the situation. Previously, we discussed the method in which you take in information and experience. Now is the time to examine the factors that cause you to avoid doing specific jobs or participating in certain social settings.

Fear of new work practises, fear of public speaking, fear of meeting new people, getting things done on time, getting jobs given to you at work, and getting jobs given to you at work are all common workplace fears.

Let's examine each one of these items in turn since it's possible that they are all on your list of things that you do not feel secure performing. The method that we will use is one that you can utilise in any given circumstance. In order for you to restore your self-assurance and learn how to emerge from your shell, each thing on the list has to be segmented into smaller, more doable chores first.

A gathering of individuals

You may not be a social butterfly, but be assured that you are not the only one who feels this way. There are a lot of individuals that avoid getting out and talking to new people. Consider the items on the list that you created about things that you like to do and that you are good at if you feel uncomfortable in this particular setting. You may use this as a way to meet others who share your interests and values. For instance, if you have an interest in photography, you may join a group dedicated to the subject. You will almost immediately find yourself surrounded by new individuals in your network of contacts who share your passion for the subject. That makes it far less awkward to talk to new individuals at any time. Imagine that you get pleasure in the kitchen. Why not host a supper at your house for a group of individuals who are familiar to you and with whom you feel at ease? This might be members of your family or other individuals that you know and trust. The greatest people to begin with are those in your circle of friends and family who are not critical of you. This will instill greater confidence in your ability to interact with others, and as time goes on, you'll be able to expand your social sphere to the point where meeting new people is no longer a challenge for you.

If you are interested in meditation and want to meet other individuals who live peaceful lives, attending a yoga class is a great way to do it. A yoga class provides you with the chance to meet individuals in an environment that is warm and inviting, and the other participants are people who, like you, are looking for ways to better themselves. The following equation can help you overcome feelings of inadequacy while interacting with new people:

Association: If you think of that person in conjunction with an activity that you take pleasure in, you won't feel awkward with them.

Find something that interests you first, and then present yourself to a place where other individuals with the same interest will be gathering. Take pleasure in the conversation.

People who have challenges with their self-esteem may find it challenging to form new connections with complete strangers; however, if you already have something in common with the other person, it makes it a lot simpler for you to practisesocialising, and you may gradually expand your social circle as your self-esteem improves.

Being Content with Being Alone

People who struggle with low self-esteem often find it impossible to take pleasure in activities as basic as spending time alone themselves. It's possible that their need for companionship is so great that it causes them to mishandle the friendships they do manage to cultivate. They have the perception that they are lacking in some way. They will never, ever acknowledge to having feelings of love for themselves and instead look for fulfilment in relationships that aren't fulfilling enough to meet their needs. When one human being becomes emotionally linked to another human being who is wounded, that person has the ability to manipulate the situation and seize control. Although in the short term this could work out for the person who has difficulties with their self-esteem, in the long run it is not going to be a healthy relationship to be in. If your lover regards you as weak and flawed, the relationship will inevitably come to an end at some point. It might go one of these two ways:

This person will not respect you and will contribute to the problems you are having with your self-esteem.

You will never be in charge of your own life because he or she will always find a way to influence you.

You have to learn to accept who you are and work on building your self-confidence because, until then, you are not ready for a serious relationship and may be putting yourself in a position to experience further sorrow. When powerful men seek for fragile women, the dominant partner will always end up dominating the dynamic, which may lead to an abusive relationship. You need to realise that these kinds of guys (or women) are not strong either; since they prey on vulnerable individuals, it indicates that they too have difficulties with self-confidence, which they then project onto another person. If your spouse has to take the lead in being strong all of the time, eventually a relationship will fail. This is because connections need to be a two-way street in equal amounts for them to be successful. In the event that they are not, there is a lack of respect, which may contribute to concerns with one's self-esteem.

Take a look at these phrases: "I need you," "I cannot live without you," and "I cannot imagine my life without you."

You need to get to the point where you are comfortable living on your own before you leap into a relationship so that you can enter the relationship as a whole and not as a dependent partner. The idea is that every human being is capable of being comfortable living on their own, and you need to get to that stage before you go into a relationship. If that is not the case, then you are not providing everything that you are capable of giving, which is not fair.

Before you get into a relationship, it is essential to work on your confidence in yourself and your abilities. others who regard themselves as individuals do not give in to the demands of others who do not respect them. In a similar vein, those who respect themselves are more likely to be respected by others. This is due to the fact that their personalities naturally attract adoration to them due to the attraction that they exude. those who don't need another person to feel whole are more likely to be able to go through life on their own terms and are less likely to be knocked down or insulted in the same manner as those who don't have any self-esteem.

Increase Your Level Of Self-Confidence By Working On Your Sense Of Self-Worth.

We are fortunate to have access to a superior option. Your other option is to focus on improving your sense of self-worth. In other words, you need to focus on changing your internalised insecurities into an externalised sense of self-assurance. When you work on yourself from the inside out to cultivate a strong foundation of self-worth and self-respect, you can then project this outside to achieve a bigger and higher degree of confidence. Is an overnight turnaround possible for this? No. Is it simple to do? However, despite the fact that it is more convenient for certain individuals than it is for others, it still involves work. However, in order to accomplish this goal, a certain degree of constancy as well as ongoing battle is necessary.

How does this thing even function?

In order to improve your self-esteem and thus your self-confidence, the first thing you need to do is alter the way in which you see yourself. You adjust the way that you look at yourself and the perspective that you have of yourself. Everyone has their own perspective on themselves. Every one of us carries about in our heads a mental image that describes who we are, what we are capable of, and where we want to go. In addition to this, we have an idea of where our place is in the overall scheme of things. In other words, we are aware of the position that we occupy in the world. People who struggle with poor self-confidence naturally have pessimistic ideas towards the aforementioned topics. They have the impression that they are at the lowest possible position. They get the impression that they do not contribute much to anything at all. They believe that no matter what they do, they will only achieve mediocrity. The fact of the matter is that they do not consider themselves to be exceptional in any way.

You need to do some work on how you see yourself. You have to alter the way in which you think about yourself. You have to shift your mindset from that of someone who is a continual victim of events and occurrences that are beyond of their control to that of someone who is someone who makes things happen. This is a huge step forward in terms of how I see myself. You go from being someone who does nothing but sit back and watch his or her life unfold in front of them to being someone who sees themselves as a person who plays a direct part in what is taking place. Again, you move from being a person who only observes what has transpired in your life with anger and asks yourself on a regular basis "what the heck happened?" to being a person who actively participates in shaping the world around them.

Everything may be connected back to how one views themselves. What kind of image do you have of yourself? How do you evaluate your own self-worth? What type of image do you have in your head when you think about yourself? This self-perception is very necessary for the process of defining oneself. When you define who you are, you also establish the boundaries of your capabilities. What you are capable of is completely up to you. You are the embodiment of either what hinders you or what propels you ahead. The most positive aspect of this whole situation is that you, and not anyone else, are in charge of determining what happens, thus you will never lose control of the situation.

Altering the Way You Tell Your Story

One further essential component of working on your self-esteem in order to increase your level of self-confidence is the need that at some time you will have to alter the story you tell yourself. As was discussed before in this book, the way you see yourself is like a never-ending tale that you tell to yourself in your head. This is the organising principle that you adhere to, or the organising tale, if you will. This story serves as a lens through which you must see all of your experiences, as well as every connection you have with other people and the wider world.

For instance, if you have a story in your head that you are an unwelcome guest and you enter through the door and people stare at you with a certain expression on their faces, it is quite probable that you would perceive that expression as a look of contempt from them. If you were to interpret the way that they stare at you as a message, you would conclude that you should not enter. You are not welcome in this place. Leave already!

If the story you tell yourself is that you are a valuable person and that other people would be delighted to have you around because you have something great to give, then you probably interpret the same glance as an invitation to introduce yourself to the other person. You might use this opportunity as a challenge to create a good first impression on the person. No matter what the circumstances are, you find yourself in a completely different location. You may choose to see it as a neutral request for interaction rather than as something that will make you feel tiny, unwanted, shut out, rejected, and irritated. It's possible that you may even look at it as a beneficial opportunity. Do you recognise the significance of the story you've created?

Your story is very important to how you make sense of the world around you because, whether you like to admit it or not, everything that we consider to be an objective fact is really a judgement. They are nothing more than that. When two individuals look at the identical collection of information, they might come to two very different conclusions about what those facts mean. The differences in these interpretations are a direct result of their respective narratives. When you work on increasing your self-confidence by focusing on your self-esteem, it is very necessary for you to change the story you tell yourself about yourself. In order for this process to function from the inside out, there needs to be certain alterations made to your own narrative.

Take The Time To Listen To Your Own Ideas

We as a whole have feelings about things that happen during our day-to-day lives. These feelings might be crippling thoughts and sentiments, or they could be specific ones. A straightforward example of checking in to your internal concerns is selecting an outfit for a special night out. You put the dress on and look in the mirror. Depending on how you feel about how you appear, you either think "wow, this dress looks amazing" or you shake your head and choose another clothing. When it comes to making the optimal decision, this is the method that requires the least amount of effort on your part to tune in to your internal thoughts or instinct.

If we are willing to be open and receptive to our inner thoughts and reflections, we may put them to countless beneficial purposes in our day-to-day lives. Our internal concerns have the potential to aid us in achieving success in the day-to-day challenges of life, growing in self-assurance, and living a life that is more pleasurable, gradually advantageous, and ultimately rewarding.

When it comes to making the right decisions and picking the right options in life, the most valuable resource you own is yourself. You thus know if something is proper and how to achieve the greatest results just by listening to your very own gut, and it sometimes lets us down. You therefore know whether something is correct and how to accomplish the finest results.

The process of tapping into your instinct is basic, and the following are some uncomplicated methods that you may start using it:

- To begin developing your instinct in the simplest manner possible, try using it to make decisions about less critical matters at first. For example, you might use it to decide what you want for dinner or which movie or café to go to.

- You will believe that it is easier to tune into yourself and your internal thoughts when it is tranquil; thus, choose a setting in which you are aware that you won't be agitated in regards to deciding on key conclusions and choices. Close your eyes, take a few deep breaths, and concentrate completely on the question at hand or the task that needs to be completed. Then, open them again and see what comes to mind right away. This is an effective method to use.

- Be ready to concede that you may make mistakes when tuning in to your instinct. While your instinct is typically correct, you may misunderstand your interior contemplations, which may lead to you making an error. • Be ready to admit that you may commit errors when tuning in to your instinct. In any case, you need to get knowledge from the errors you commit and maintain the process of developing and enhancing your internal direction. Don't complicate things by making an effort or trying to influence the suitable response in some manner while you're allowing your inner guidance a chance to come through. Chances are, if you're leaning towards moving in a certain path, you probably already know the answer to your question.

Following the steps above is the easiest way to get your internal guidance to start coming to the surface when you need it, and the more you go to it and utilise it, the easier it will become. Follow your heart, your own thoughts and feelings, and you will never stray too far from the right path. This is the advice that the animated character "Jiminy Cricket" gave to his friend Pinocchio in the song "consistently let you still, small voice be your guide." It is precisely at the moment that we begin to lose confidence and confusion about ourselves that we get unstuck and reluctant, which ultimately causes us to veer off course or come to a halt.

Get What You Can Out Of Your Relationships

According to the findings of the research on adult life that has been ongoing for 75 years, the most important factor in leading a happier and healthier life is having positive interactions with other people. For an introvert who only sometimes communicates with one or two of his close friends, this may seem to be disappointing news. Fortunately, it does not matter how many friends we have; what matters is the quality of the interactions we have with those friends. Because of this, we are in a better position than before. People who are more introverted tend to be specialists at developing meaningful and long-lasting relationships.

However, despite the fact that we have characteristics that are beneficial to a healthy relationship, we also have those that are destructive to it. It is necessary for us to evaluate each of our connections to see whether or not we are working to improve them.

What characteristics contribute to the success of your relationships?

Being able to listen attentively -Even introverts have a natural need to speak about themselves, but it's hard to find someone who really listens to what they have to say. For this reason, attentive listeners are valuable companions, particularly for an introvert who is often the one to perform the listening.

You have the capacity for meaningful discourse.Conversations that go farther lead to relationships that go further. Even the most outgoing people like having meaningful conversations with others. They are able to speak freely on weighty matters because they are certain that their words will be regarded seriously. In addition, the researchers discovered that the happiest individuals are those that prioritise having interactions that are important above those that are superficial.

Your tendency to reflect deeply before acting means that you almost never find yourself wishing you could take back anything you've said. Continue to watch what you say since thoughtless words may severely harm even the most intimate of relationships.

Your inclination for a more intimate and close-knit circle of friends — A smaller circle of friends ensures more connection and commitment. Aside from that, it's impossible for humans to keep more than a few close relationships going at once. Because of this, some friendships come to an end as others begin. When you have fewer friends, you tend to hold on to the ones you do have for longer, which in turn makes them more precious. Introverts, by nature, have a strong sense of loyalty to the few close friends they do have.

Which of your characteristics puts a strain on your relationships?

Passive listening occurs when we fail to reply to the person who is speaking because we are too preoccupied with listening to them or thinking about what they are saying. Interject a few questions or comments to demonstrate that you are paying attention.

Reticent nature–It's not always a negative thing to be reserved, but there are instances when we leave too many things unsaid, including comments that convey our care for one another. Get out of your rut and try something new. There may be moments when you have to make concessions for the benefit of the people and causes that are important to you.

By avoiding conflicts, you may be able to maintain the peace for the time being; nonetheless, this behaviour is subtly damaging your relationship. You will need to push yourself outside of your comfort zone once again in order to succeed in this endeavour. It is always possible to confront someone in a reasonable and calm manner.

We have a propensity to be too critical and judgemental, and this, along with our reluctance to open up to new people, makes it difficult for us to make new acquaintances. Try to keep in mind that not all of our assessments are correct. It's best to assume the best of other people. The majority of the time, the person we least anticipate becoming friends with is the one we do wind up befriending.

Avoid surprising your pals by suddenly becoming unreachable by informing them in advance of any time you intend to recharge your batteries. Because being alone has the opposite impact on extroverts, your friends who are extroverts may not grasp the need of it if you don't take the time to explain it to them.

Participate in low-key social gatherings.

It's true that being with other people may be draining for introverts, but it's also true that we love the time we get to spend with other people. The simple act of striking up a chat with a kind stranger or exchanging pleasantries with a bubbly cashier may do wonders for our spirits. Even for someone who is naturally an introvert, researchers discovered that good feelings might be triggered by taking a more outgoing or forceful stance.

When we interact with other people, we experience an increase in happiness, just like everyone else. The only real difference is that our energy is depleted, but extroverts' is replenished when they interact with others. So, how exactly may we profit by interacting with other people? Do we have to exert ourselves to our physical and mental limits every time we want to experience joy?

The following are some methods in which you may maintain your social connections without making sacrifices:

Find others who share your values and perspectives. When you spend time with another introvert, you understand one other's limits and sensitivity, which makes the experience less tiring overall.

Engage others in brief but meaningful exchanges. For example, you may approach the shop clerk and inquire about her day. Being forceful is starting the conversation with someone else.

Spend time and energy on the people who are most important to you. Just being in their company may help you feel more at ease and certain of who you are. They have acknowledged you in your natural state, thus you should do the same.

Reading a book or following a blog provides you with the necessary social connection, despite the fact that they are solitary activities. It is even possible for it to be more personal than a brief talk. Reading enables one to get a glimpse into another person's private emotions and thoughts.

Growing one's own sense of self-worth is directly linked to enhanced social skills.

People who have healthy levels of self-confidence often exude a sense of calm and ease whether they are in a social setting or during a first encounter engagement. When a person has self-confidence, their trust in themselves comes from inside and is not influenced by the opinions of others. This allows them to thrive in any situation. People that are able to do this are able to proceed through social situations stress-free since they are not worried about being rejected. Psychologists have shown that when individuals are confronted with a task, they feel more at ease if they have high levels of self-confidence. People who are self-assured have a sense of excitement for their future and are more at ease when expressing this excitement to others. Because they are more self-assured and enthusiastic, they conduct themselves in the same manner and are able to have discussions that are more animated and flow more easily as a result. People who are confident feel more at ease in a variety of social circumstances, and this quality attracts a lot of attention from other people because it makes them seem more approachable. They tend to exude a good aura that is not only very appealing but also easily spreadable to others around them.

It's possible that some individuals may claim that a person's self-assurance in social settings is more significant than their self-assurance in challenging academic settings. The most significant aspects of our life, such as employment, relationships, and opportunities, are often awarded to those who have higher levels of social competence. The majority of employers put a higher value on a person's emotional intelligence than they do on their IQ, according to the findings of a lot of recent study that was carried out in the contemporary workplace. When hiring managers are in the process of hiring a candidate but have to choose between one who has more experience but is less emotionally intelligent compared to another candidate who has less experience but is more emotionally intelligent, they will frequently hire the candidate that has more emotional intelligence. This is because hiring managers believe that emotional intelligence is more important than experience in determining a candidate's suitability for a position. This is given a higher priority due to the significance that virtually all companies put on maintaining strong personal connections. A person's level of self-assurance has a direct bearing on their capacity to perform well in social contexts and is an asset to them when it comes to forming and cultivating connections. In the end, given that more professions involve some kind of human connection, a person who is able to more successfully create and develop relationships will have a greater chance of being successful. This is because more jobs require some form of human interaction.

Because of our basic human inclinations, the majority of individuals are naturally drawn to those who exude greater levels of self-confidence. In the distant past, our predecessors who had the healthiest bodies were most likely also the ones who possessed the highest levels of self-assurance. People who had the highest levels of physical fitness and self-confidence were often given leadership roles, and as a result, more individuals were drawn to them. It's possible that when humans progressed into the contemporary day, our attraction to a person's physical appearance changed, but our attraction to the way they carry themselves remained the same. People will always be attracted to those that exude self-assurance and have a natural tendency to treat others with greater respect.

Putting Your Objectives Down In Writing On Paper

Goal-setting worksheets are efficient tools that will guide you through every step of the goal-setting process and assist you in formulating a strategy that will increase the chances of your dream becoming a reality. These worksheets may be found online or in printed form.

1. Creating a goal-setting worksheet will make it easier for you to see the larger picture. They are wonderful tools for visualising the future and seeing yourself, or who you have the potential to become, in a few years' time in the future. They may help guide your thoughts and life patterns in a certain direction so that you can make decisions that are appropriate in light of your ultimate objective.

2. Completing a goal-setting worksheet can assist you in defining your objectives as well as determining the reasons "why" these specific objectives are significant. The forms will guide you through particular steps that will require you to think about your vision, your priorities, and your end goal as they are being completed. In order for a goal to be meaningful to you, it is necessary for it to be meaningful to others. You will have a more in-depth understanding of yourself, and as a result, you will be able to bring more clarity and focus to the accomplishment of your objectives.

3. Creating a goal-setting worksheet can assist you in partitioning your overall objective into more manageable sub-goals and steps. Understanding the larger picture is essential because, before you can start your journey, you need to have a clear idea of where you

want to end up. On the other hand, the journey from where you are to where you want to be may sometimes seem quite daunting.

The form enables you to set both short-term and long-term goals, which, when combined, will assist you in realising your ambitions one step at a time. You may divide a long-term goal into annual, monthly, weekly, and even daily goals; after all, we are capable of doing anything if we take it one day at a time, isn't that right?

You will be asked by the work sheet to list the steps that are necessary to accomplish your strategy and to prioritise your actions in order to achieve success.

4. The goal-setting worksheets that you use will assist you in developing a plan of action and determining the requirements that are necessary to

pursue your goal. To accomplish a goal, especially one that is more ambitious or has a longer time frame, requires careful planning.

By laying out the steps that need to be taken in order for you to realise your goals. You will be aware of all that has to be done and will be able to approach your objective from a very realistic point of view. You will also be able to identify any potential obstacles with the help of this form. This will allow you to be better prepared to deal with any issues that may arise and prevent any unpleasant surprises.

This is especially important if you have a shared goal that you are working towards with someone else, such as a partner in business or a team. Other examples of shared goals include a partnership and a group project. A goal-setting worksheet will detail the duties of each individual and ensure that everyone is on the same page with regard to both the overall objective and the plan of action.

5. Goal-setting worksheets provide accountability and make it possible to track your progress towards achieving your objectives. Because life has a lot of distractions and it is often easy to lose sight of what you are working towards, it is tremendously beneficial to have a clear goal in mind at all times. must have a method for monitoring your progress and keeping track of it.

Make it a habit to check your worksheets on a regular basis and cross off any goals that you have already achieved. Recognising and appreciating your successes can increase your sense of self-worth and encourage you to keep going despite setbacks or discouragement you may have along the way.

Continuous monitoring will not only help you identify where you went wrong but will also help you adjust or revise your course of action as necessary along the way. Keep in mind that your plan has not yet been etched in stone. It will provide you with direction and a framework within which to operate, but there may be times when circumstances need you to be flexible or make changes that will improve your plan of action. In these cases, you should be prepared to adapt your plan accordingly.

6. Creating a goal-setting worksheet will boost your chances of success and speed up the process of reaching your objectives. You will be able to maintain your focus and motivation if you have a well-defined plan, especially if your "short-term goals" are attainable,

measurable, and provide you the opportunity to celebrate your successes on a regular basis.

Many people never accomplish what they set out to do because they lack the knowledge necessary to turn their dreams into a reality. The forms give clarity and focus, allowing you to understand precisely what is required of you on a daily, weekly, or monthly basis. You will have an easier time sticking to the plan and seeing it through to completion if you have a crystal clear understanding of the steps you should do.

7. A work sheet for goal setting should include time periods and due dates. A fantastic recipe for success involves partitioning big goals into more manageable sections, identifying the steps that need to be followed, and

establishing a deadline for their completion.

Setting a deadline for yourself is the most effective way to transform procrastination into motivation. You could even find that being accountable to someone who will check to ensure that you have fulfilled your time frame guideline is beneficial to you.

You will gain direction, remain motivated and focused, and experience an increase in self-confidence as you monitor your progress towards achieving your goals after writing them down and committing them to paper.

Take The Time To Listen To Your Own Ideas.

We as a whole have feelings about things that happen during our day-to-day lives. These feelings might be crippling thoughts and sentiments, or they could be specific ones. A straightforward example of checking in to your internal concerns is selecting an outfit for a special night out. You put the dress on and look in the mirror. Depending on how you feel about how you appear, you either think "wow, this dress looks amazing" or you shake your head and choose another clothing. When it comes to making the optimal decision, this is the method that requires the least amount of effort on your part to tune in to your internal thoughts or instinct.

If we are willing to be open and receptive to our inner thoughts and reflections, we may put them to countless beneficial purposes in our day-to-day lives. Our internal concerns have the potential to aid us in achieving success in the day-to-day challenges of life, growing in self-assurance, and living a life that is more pleasurable, gradually advantageous, and ultimately rewarding.

When it comes to making the right decisions and picking the right options in life, the most valuable resource you own is yourself. You thus know if something is proper and how to achieve the greatest results just by listening to your very own gut, and it sometimes lets us down. You therefore know whether something is correct and how to accomplish the finest results.

The process of tapping into your instinct is basic, and the following are some uncomplicated methods that you may start using it:

- To begin developing your instinct in the simplest manner possible, try using it to make decisions about less critical matters at first. For example, you might use it to decide what you want for dinner or which movie or café to go to.

- You will believe that it is easier to tune into yourself and your internal thoughts when it is tranquil; thus, choose a setting in which you are aware that you won't be agitated in regards to deciding on key conclusions and choices. Close your eyes, take a few deep breaths, and concentrate completely on the question at hand or the task that needs to be completed. Then, open them again and see what comes to mind right away. This is an effective method to use.

- Be ready to concede that you may make mistakes when tuning in to your instinct. While your instinct is typically correct, you may misunderstand your interior contemplations, which may lead to you making an error. • Be ready to admit that you may commit errors when tuning in to your instinct. In any case, you need to get knowledge from the errors you commit and maintain the process of developing and enhancing your internal direction.

• Don't complicate things by making an effort or trying to influence the suitable response in some manner while you're allowing your inner guidance a chance to come through. Chances are, if you're leaning towards moving in a certain path, you probably already know the answer to your question.

Following the steps above is the easiest way to get your internal guidance to start coming to the surface when you need it, and the more you go to it and utilise it, the easier it will become. Follow your heart, your own thoughts and feelings, and you will never stray too far from the right path. This is the advice that the animated character "Jiminy Cricket" gave to his friend Pinocchio in the song "consistently let you still, small voice be your guide." It is precisely at the moment that we begin to lose confidence and confusion about ourselves that we get unstuck and reluctant, which ultimately causes us to veer off course or come to a halt.

Visualisation in the mind helps.

Something that everyone of us already has, namely our one-of-a-kind creative minds, is one of the most influential and motivating tools that can be used on a daily basis, and it may be used to great effect. You may make use of your very own considerations, tidbits of information, ideas, and instincts in your day-to-day existence to roll out good improvements for the better in any aspect of your life. Everyone has a creative mind, but some of us have one that is more unique and that comes to life more quickly than others do. However, with a little bit of practise, all of us would be able to construct symbols in our minds that would work to our advantage.

Put your creative energy to good use.

You are the only one who can restrict how you use your creative mind to benefit you in your day-to-day life. You can use your creative mind to visualise any number of things and apply it for almost any occasion. The process of representation involves creating a favourable mental picture of the outcome of a set of events, visualising this favourable outcome in your brain at the same moment it is taking place, and allowing this favourable outcome the opportunity to supplant any unfavourable thoughts that you may have been having.

You need to build up the perception as much as you can and look at it from all angles and points of view. The mental image that you develop in your mind has to be as clear as possible of how you want the situation to turn out. Consider your imaginative thinking and the mental image you work with as a blueprint for developing and building on, similar to the way a modeller uses a schematic when planning a job all the way through. Think about how you may use this to your advantage.

The basis of everything

Establish the frames of your concept or what it is that you desire to change in your viewpoint first, and then progressively build from the base, plainly envisioning each and every nook and corner of the thought. The foundational work that lies behind your thinking is the cause for your success. When deciding how to rest the businesses, keep the accompanying in mind.

• Exactly what is it that I need to work on or alter, and how can I do that?

• What kind of a difference will this cause to create?

• Will my own efforts be sufficient to meet my requirements?

• What do I need to find out about how to do this? • What kinds of changes do I need to make in my life in order to accomplish this?

When you have established the frameworks for whatever it is that you wish to change in your life, you can then feel free to develop on your arrangement, envision the project at all times as would be prudent, and see the entire undertaking from beginning to end work in your mind as precisely as could be allowed. If you want to find a way to achieve what it is that you want, once you have the perception finished in your mind, then you can find a way to accomplish what it is that you want. If you want to find a way to accomplish what it is that you want, then write down the steps you took in your mind and make a hard copy of them in order to achieve the result, and then complete these steps in their entirety.

Superior Capabilities In The Field Of Entrepreneurship

Entrepreneurs would do well to develop their intuitive faculties and improve their problem-solving skills; empaths make excellent businesspeople. They have a laser-like concentration on providing the very best outcomes for their customers, irrespective of the industry in which those customers operate. In addition, they are strongly motivated by the need to have independence and to get away from the poisonous, overpowering, and greedy settings of regular 9 to 5 occupations. This desire drives them.

Entrepreneurs with empathy are particularly adept at conceiving up novel businesses that cater to the requirements of their customers in ways that bigger corporations are more likely to entirely ignore. They often establish their own businesses, which are geared towards bringing about some kind of social transformation or healing in today's world. Empaths often pursue careers as counsellors, life and business coaches, alternative healers, artists, authors, and a variety of other professions. Empaths also frequently select these types of careers. Fortunately, each of them may be approached as a business opportunity in and of itself. They are also ideal selections because they cater to the specific abilities and limitations of the empath, enabling the empath to shine as brightly as they possibly can while also allowing them to serve in the manner in which their soul requires them to shine.

If you are an empath and you are not already on the route of becoming an entrepreneur, you may discover that commencing this life path brings you a great deal of pleasure and value. You have the potential to launch your life as an entrepreneur and achieve a high level of success in that endeavour because to the skills and qualities you possess. The decision to pursue this line of work comes with a number of significant advantages. A few examples of these advantages are as follows:

When opposed to having a job, having no employment gives you a significant increase in the amount of freedom and flexibility you have in your life.

You are in charge of determining your own work schedule as well as vacation time.

You do not have to put up with the exhausting and hazardous conditions that come with a typical 9 to 5 work.

You are free to collaborate with anybody you like, or you may opt to do all of your work online.

You have the option to work from home, where you have the ability to make far more money than you would in a traditional job.

You have the opportunity to put your creative skills to good use.

Develop a sense of accomplishment and contentment in the work that you perform.

It's possible that you'll have access to more travel options.

When you remove yourself from toxic and negative work situations, you will notice an improvement in your general health and happiness.

A lot of people think that empathetic entrepreneurship is going to be the most successful business model in the future. huge firms and corporations are often renowned for being reckless, rude, and brutal in their commercial dealings. As more and more individuals want to lead lives that are more socially aware and responsible, more of them are avoiding doing business with huge businesses and organisations. These very same individuals are looking for company owners that are operating their own socially responsible companies in a manner that satisfies their requirements on a personal level in a true and authentic way. Because you are an empath, you already possess all of the skills necessary to serve in this capacity, which means that these individuals are seeking for someone just like you and your abilities.

Powerful Connections to Both Animals and Plants

Empaths have a special connection with both plants and animals, which is another one of their many impressive abilities. You may already be familiar with animal empaths and plant empaths, and you may also be aware of the extraordinary abilities that these types of people possess when it comes to interacting with animals and plants. In a world in which very little regard has been given to the environment and the people who live it, this comes as a welcome and much-needed breath of fresh air. In today's contemporary society, many people seldom think about other people of their own species, much alone other species or living forms. You may have a tremendous capacity as an empath to connect to these living forms and defend them from the harm caused by people who feel very little or no empathy in their lives. If this is the case, you are an empath.

It is thought that animals and plants are empathetic as well, which means that you can discover that animals and plants react favourably to you as well. It's possible that you'll be able to bring animals into your life and have an unusual capacity to make plants flourish in a manner that other people would have trouble doing. This is due to the fact that they are perceptive and can tell when you are being charitable. Because of this, they will naturally trust you and will experience feelings of being secure, protected, and fed while they are in your company. They pick up on your enthusiasm, and they attribute their success in part to it.

Instruments That Can Help A Person Become More Self-Aware

Emotional intelligence absolutely relies on one's level of self-awareness. It is necessary to acquire a somewhat in-depth grasp of oneself before moving on to the task of comprehending another person. To begin, you should examine your degree of self-awareness by posing a few questions to yourself in order to determine whether or not it is enough. Ask yourself, "What difficulties have I encountered in my life?" Your narrative will reveal what you believe about your life, and this may serve as an indication of the degree to which you are self-aware. If your response is anything along the lines of "I'm not really sure; I had a pretty typical childhood," then you are not alone. If you have ever found yourself saying something like, "I got this job kind of by luck; I am not really sure about my future," then this will tell you all you need to know. You are a person who has not fully incorporated the events of your life into who you are as an individual. It's possible that you won't feel like you have a purpose or direction in life, or that you won't understand why you do the things that you do.

A response that is more self-aware may go something like this: "I am a man who is 32 years old and was born in the Pacific Northwest, but I moved to California for college." As a brilliant and capable programmer, I was given a range of jobs; but, I chose the one I have today since it appeared to be the greatest choice out of all of the possibilities. Soon, I'm hoping to find someone with whom I'll be able to start a family. This is a more thoughtful and straightforward response. It seems as if the individual who provided this response is aware of both who he is and where he wants to go in the future.

Regrettably, self-awareness is not something that can be purposefully attained by an individual. It is something that, like to knowledge, can only be gained with age and experience. The easiest method to increase your level of self-awareness is to sometimes go outside of yourself and engage in activities or situations that are in contrast to what you are generally used to. For instance, if you have never listened to a certain kind of music before, you need to give it a go to determine whether or not it is something you would like. This will provide you with some background and information on the sort of music you like listening to as well as the reasons why you favour that style of music over others.

Sometimes we get too used to where we are in many different ways, and as a result, we lose the will to make changes. Although this is a human situation that may be understood, it cannot be the one that we continue to live with as we go ahead in our lives. We have to force ourselves to go outside of our comfort zones. I have no doubt that you have heard anything similar to this before. The majority of individuals are just unaware of how simple it is to go outside of their comfort zone. You could decide to go for a trip downtown with a few of your close friends even if downtown is a bit of a distance away and you do not often feel like travelling for such a long distance. That is not a problem! You have the ability to succeed. Experiment with anything that deviates from your typical routine; doing so will help you become more self-aware since it will expose you to new experiences that might widen your perspective.

There are a lot of things you can do to expose yourself to new experiences, and I encourage you to try as many of them as you can. You may, for instance, start a whole new activity for yourself. Perhaps playing an instrument in a band is something that has always been on your bucket list. Taking up this pastime won't be too difficult for you if you invest in a low-cost instrument and make use of the materials available on the internet. This will not only provide you a new channel for expression, but it will also present you with mental challenges that will help keep your mind flexible and focused.

An knowledge of behaviourism and, in particular, the structure of the reward system in relation to the reinforcement and punishment of certain behaviours is another one of the fundamental tools and characteristics for doing a person analysis. This is because behaviourism focuses on how certain actions are rewarded and punished. This is done in behaviourism in order to investigate the phenomena of how we learn new things. According to behaviourism, the way we learn is mostly determined by rewards and punishments, which are doled out in accordance with our actions. When we are rewarded for behaviour in whatever manner, whether it is an emotional release or a physical satisfaction, such as eating a piece of candy, we do that activity again. This is true whether the reward is an emotional release or a physical enjoyment. When there is a consequence for a certain activity, we have a tendency to avoid engaging in that behaviour whenever it is feasible. This is the primary driving force behind our education as human and animal animals, and at times, it may be far more convoluted than it may first seem. For instance, the physical action of running is associated with a certain psychological perk in the brain. When we put up a significant amount of effort, such as when we go for a run or engage in any other physically taxing activity, certain feel-good chemicals are released in our brains. Because of this, you could be led to believe that humans have a natural propensity towards running and other forms of physical exercise, right? Yes, but we also have a built-in propensity to be swayed by the opinions and ideas of other people and objects. For example, the reward of sugar is a strong sensation of pleasure, and occasionally we might get addicted to that feeling of pleasure. Additionally, there is the discomfort and difficulty that comes along with jogging when you are not in the finest of condition, which acts as a parallel punishment for the exercise because of how it affects your body. If a person is mentally capable of comprehending the fact that when they run, they will feel some pain but will feel far better later, then they will be much more successful. They will have the knowledge necessary to engage in the activity in order to get the desired end reward.

There are some conditions, such as long-term addiction, that have the potential to alter the way the brain functions. The brain begins to get a hold of the same material over and over again, whether it is sugar or fat or happiness from porn or whatever else, and it starts to become acclimated to it as a reward. This may happen whether the substance being sought after is happiness from porn or sugar or fat or whatever else. However, after some time has passed, these reward centres get exhausted, and they eventually stop seeing the drugs in question as a source of reward.

Following this, the brain begins to regard the compulsion's target not at all as a source of pleasure. Despite this, the individual continues to participate in the activity on a consistent basis. The individual is stuck in a rut in which they are driven to continue participating in the activity even if they are no longer obtaining the benefit for doing so. This is a frequent condition that many individuals get into after engaging in a wide variety of activities and using a variety of drugs.

To be able to grasp the components of their early development and family of origin that came with their lives is another crucial talent in the task of improving emotional intelligence. This is because these characteristics came with them throughout their lives. This is significant because the family in which we were raised is the environment in which we initially develop all of the ways in which we interact with the outside world and how we are in the outside world. These are the kinds of individuals that serve as models for us as we come of age. They serve as models for us of what masculinity and femininity seem like in our everyday lives. They are, in point of fact, illustrative models of all of the behaviours that we first comprehend. Because individuals do not mature in a sterile environment, it is only via this prism that we can fully comprehend the reasons behind people's actions. They are raised around flawed individuals who are prone to making errors and who cannot be predicted.

The practise of emotional intelligence requires a number of skills, one of which is visual observation. Visual observation will provide you with the tools necessary to examine body language and decipher the genuine intentions of other people. It will also assist you in evaluating facial expressions, personal cleanliness, the clothing choices individuals make, and other visual indicators.

Increasing One's Level Of Self-Assurance Is Associated With An Increase In Overall Happiness.

while a person has a healthy degree of self-confidence, they naturally feel more confident while they are doing activities, which eventually leads to a greater success rate; as a result, they are able to feel good about themselves, which ultimately leads to more self-confidence, which finally leads to more happiness. Individuals who make their living participating in self-esteem-boosting programmes and courses People who are happier and have more life satisfaction tend to exhibit greater levels of self-confidence, according to several reports.

People who have a higher level of self-confidence have a tendency to take on the world with a greater level of ferocity and conviction. This, in turn, enables them to have a greater sense of connection with their surroundings, and they naturally feel a higher level of contentment and security in their relationships. Naturally, they also have a greater power to influence others, and they have the abilities to regulate both their own behaviours and emotions in a more compelling manner. This is because they have the ability to control themselves in a more compelling manner. Because of this, effective leaders across the globe tend to have greater levels of self-confidence. This, in turn, garners respect from their followers in a natural manner and ultimately results in a working atmosphere that is both healthier and more functional. Confidence is extremely similar to self-esteem in the sense that when a person has a more positive attitude towards themselves and the world around them, they have a higher level of self-esteem.

The notion of what brings about pleasure is one of the least well known topics in the whole universe. When asked about the source of their pleasure, most individuals would respond with one of the following:

Getting a better career, Buying a better automobile, Finding a significant other, Having a kid, Having more money, and Purchasing a nicer home are some goals that people often have.

There is a consistent thread running through all of those responses, and that is the fact that virtually all of them are materialistic. Neither having things nor purchasing things can bring about satisfaction on their own. When a person has too many stuff, it may often lead to misery, which is the reverse consequence of what one would expect from having more possessions. The capacity of a person to comprehend their own internal nature and to maintain a lifestyle that is congruent with that comprehension is the true secret to that person's contentment. If you are able to identify the aspects of your life that are most important to you, you will be in a better position to formulate a strategy that will lead you to your goals. You need to motivate yourself through building up your sense of self-worth in order to accomplish those goals. A person must have self-confidence in order to recognise what adjustments or compromises they will need to make in order to attain the goals they have set for themselves, which are outlined in the list that was just presented. If a person does not have faith in this, they are likely to have feelings of disorientation, helplessness, and confusion about why life isn't fair and why they are unable to have the things that other people do.

Growing one's own sense of self-worth is directly linked to enhanced social skills.

People who have healthy levels of self-confidence often exude a sense of calm and ease whether they are in a social setting or during a first encounter engagement. When a person has self-confidence, their trust in themselves comes from inside and is not influenced by the opinions of others. This allows them to thrive in any situation. People that are able to do this are able to proceed through social situations stress-free since they are not worried about being rejected. Psychologists have shown that when individuals are confronted with a task, they feel more at ease if they have high levels of self-confidence. People who are self-assured have a sense of excitement for their future and are more at ease when expressing this excitement to others. Because they are more self-assured and enthusiastic, they conduct themselves in the same manner and are able to have discussions that are more animated and flow more easily as a result. People who are confident feel more at ease in a variety of social circumstances, and this quality attracts a lot of attention from other people because it makes them seem more approachable. They tend to exude a good aura that is not only very appealing but also easily spreadable to others around them.

It's possible that some individuals may claim that a person's self-assurance in social settings is more significant than their self-assurance in challenging academic settings. The most significant aspects of our life, such as employment, relationships, and opportunities, are often awarded to those who have higher levels of social competence. The majority of employers put a higher value on a person's emotional intelligence than they do on their IQ, according to the findings of a lot of recent study that was carried out in the contemporary workplace. When hiring managers are in the process of hiring a candidate but have to choose between one who has more experience but is less emotionally intelligent compared to another candidate who has less experience but is more emotionally intelligent, they will frequently hire the candidate that has more emotional intelligence. This is because hiring managers believe that emotional intelligence is more important than experience in determining a candidate's suitability for a position. This is given a higher priority due to the significance that virtually all companies put on maintaining strong personal connections. A person's level of self-assurance has a direct bearing on their capacity to perform well in social contexts and is an asset to them when it comes to forming and cultivating connections. In the end, given that more professions involve some kind of human connection, a person who is able to more successfully create and develop relationships will have a greater chance of being successful. This is because more jobs require some form of human interaction.

Because of our basic human inclinations, the majority of individuals are naturally drawn to those who exude greater levels of self-confidence. In the distant past, our predecessors who had the healthiest bodies were most likely also the ones who possessed the highest levels of self-assurance. People who had the highest levels of physical fitness and self-confidence were often given leadership roles, and as a result, more individuals were drawn to them. It's possible that when humans progressed into the contemporary day, our attraction to a person's physical appearance changed, but our attraction to the way they carry themselves remained the same. People will always be attracted to those that exude self-assurance and have a natural tendency to treat others with greater respect.

Smart Methods For Maintaining Your Motivation

If you have ever attempted to achieve a goal or realise a dream, you are well aware that just having the desire to do so is not sufficient. It's simple to fall in love with whatever it is that you want, but getting what you want isn't exactly a walk in the park. It doesn't matter what it is that you want; falling in love with it is simple. The motivation, as well as your own personal motives, become relevant at this point in the discussion.

When you first started desiring anything, all you could see was your desire for the item you desired and the object itself. The psychological awakening to all of the challenges that await you along your chosen path does not take place all at once. Because humans are, at heart, social animals, these things occur in the sequence that they do for that very reason. We take in what we see, we want it, and it comes to us. The end of the story.

However, in real life, this principle isn't always applicable. In real life, in addition to concepts like "struggle," "competition," and "hindrance," there are many other concepts that come into play. Every single item is a smack in the face for the psyche.

The mind, which naively believed that just desiring something was enough, gradually comes to the realisation that there are a lot of other factors working against it. It starts to see the 'price' it has to pay in order to achieve the goal it has set for itself.

The motives are beginning to lose their initial charm in a way that is gradual but steady. The want is still very much there, but for some reason that is beyond my understanding, the drive appears to have disappeared. Mind you, the desire is still very much there. Suddenly, the only thing that is left is the portion where you want it. The reason for this, ladies and gentlemen, is that motivation has long since left the building.

If you remember well, the definition of motivation is that it "implies two things," namely a change in behaviour as well as the existence of a reason. This is quite clear. The moment each of these things comes to an end, motivation also comes to an end.

Now, at long last, we are able to discuss the most important and thought-provoking aspect of this whole narrative: "How does one remain motivated?"

The question that costs a million dollars. How can one ensure that they do not lose track of the objective and continue to go forward without losing their drive?

The correct response is, thankfully, a lot less dramatic and a lot simpler to comprehend and put into practise. The following are a few of the most tried and tested ways that have been shown to be effective in maintaining motivation regardless of the circumstances.

1. Put the objective in writing.

How often have you begun anything with enough drive to conquer the world, only to find that less than a week later you are asking yourself, "Why did I even begin doing this in the first place?" What should you do if you find that you are unable to recall the reason? You, it is fairly obvious, are out.

We believe that if we are unable to recall a particular reason, it is most likely because the reason was not compelling enough in the first place. That, my good friend, is the first step towards falling short of one's goals.

As soon as you have an objective in mind, strip away all of the ancillary details that are in the background, and then jot down the primary motivation behind why you are doing or are going to accomplish it. Don't leave any space for interpretation. When you look at that piece of paper and read your goal, it has to be crystal obvious, and it needs to get you where it needs to go you (in your heart)!

2. Divide and conquer has been a winning strategy for the most powerful leaders in the history of the world from the beginning of time itself. This tactic was used by everyone from Julius Caesar and the Roman Empire to the British Empire. Then there is no reason for us not to.

The expression "Rome was not built in a day" is a well-known proverb.

It highlights how important it is to be patient and give things some time. Getting into something is simple, but getting out of it is more difficult. You must first get an understanding of the many stages that will be required in order to accomplish your objective, and then break each step down into more manageable chunks of time.

Take, for instance, your decision to shed 10 kilogrammes as an example. One day is not going to be enough time to accomplish this goal using the method of consistent exercise and nutrition. In the vast majority of cases, it will not occur within the next month either.

But if you plan it out carefully and break it down into smaller, more manageable goals, such as dropping 1 kilogramme every five to seven days, you have a decent chance of losing 10 kilogrammes in two months, and maybe even more.

Therefore, the idea is straightforward. Break the process of reaching your final objective down into manageable periods. Then, one by one, you'll be able to bring down all of the tep and win the battle.

3. Be aware of and be open to any and all possible outcomes.

To sum it up in a single word, I want you to be sensible.

The majority of the time, we don't have enough motivation because we don't realise that certain things aren't going to happen no matter what we do. Those things are unavoidable. There is a potential weakness in our plan that might prevent us from achieving our objective. However, this does not mean that we will cease our efforts.

In a difficult test, your goal is to get the highest possible ranking. Are you going to give up just because there's a chance that someone else, somewhere, has a photographic memory and is also going to take the same test? To your knowledge, no.

In that spirit, you need to have an open mind and be ready for anything that may come your way. You could go very close to winning yet end up losing anyhow. Or you might have a good chance of losing but yet end up with a victory in the end!

Why should that be discounted?

4. Let go of the pessimists

There is an old proverb that goes, "A pessimist is someone who, when they smell flowers, begin looking for a grave!"

If someone has already made up their mind that they are going to fail, there is no one, and I repeat, no one who can help them. You may turn a horse that is losing a race into a winner by giving him enough encouragement and support, but a horse who refuses to run has no future. The sickness of pessimism has the ability to transform even the most capable individual into someone who is completely worthless. Therefore, there is truly no room for motivation in a mind that breeds pessimistic thought since there is no room for it.

As soon as you adopt a positive outlook, you'll find that motivation is right on your heels.

5. Surround yourself with things that will inspire you.

It is only natural that you will experience feelings of depression if you are in the company of unhappy, moping people for an extended period of time. It's not rocket science; it's just common sense. If you surround yourself with people who are successful, happy, motivated, and full of energy, you will discover that some of those traits will rub off on you. Simply because the human mind is a mimicking machine. When the mind perceives ad, it experiences ad as a feeling. It is happy when it sees other people happy.

You will, unless you are a sadist or masochist, discover that you automatically feel invigorated when you are in the company of the energetic. This is true even if you are a masochist. Read books on how to encourage yourself, as well as biographies of people who have achieved a lot in their lives. Listening to music with a quick beat is also helpful in this regard.

6. Quit making excuses for yourself.

Motivation is like that wonderful friend that, when they leave the party, people start to follow them. When you feel motivated, others start to follow you.

But you assert that "No" one will depart after the party is over. Why?

Because you need the party to end so that you can start having fun at the after-party!

You need to stop looking for reasons to get out of the game and start looking for reasons to keep playing it. If you have five primary motives to begin with, you should add five more motives that will serve as "After-Party Motives." Maintain a straightforward policy. In this game, if you sleep, you lose. You have to put up the effort to get whatever it is that you want. Therefore, get yourself up, wipe the cobwebs from your eyes, and get the after-party started!

Maintain an awareness of your ego. Our deeper selves prefer to take control of our lives and steer the course of events, but only if and until we are able to expose them for who and what they really are. By remembering it, you stop the personality from taking over and becoming dominant. Your ego needs to be able to take control of a room, dominate a conversation, feel dominating, and own your personality. Be conscious of the fact that the ego is the source of your feelings of superiority, judgement, and hostility. Always be on the lookout for evidence of the inner self, and use this information to your advantage as you try to win the affection of the elusive creature.

Take responsibility for what you say. Be deliberate and insufficient with your use of language. Be aware that words have the power to harm. If there is an alternative way to phrase it that would be easier on someone's ears and heart, then you should try to phrase it in a more pleasant way. If there is a way to converse that causes less harm and more movement, then you should choose that strategy. Consider opting for silence instead of words if the situation calls for something more subdued. Words have meanings, and those meanings have consequences. Be familiar with the language that you use.

Replace anger with admiration to calm the situation. Be glad to see the fury when it reaches the point when it explodes like a volcano spewing lava. Observe it while it repeatedly cleans to obtain a better understanding of the source of your aggravation. Make plans to sit with your anger for a while so that you can find out how to deal with it more effectively. When you don't receive what you want, anger quickly follows. Or, on the other side, when someone is unable to fulfil your expectations or causes you to feel disappointment. Awakening to the reality that nobody can make you angry is a necessary step. Nobody except you can understand the things that set you off and make you frustrated. Do you feel as if in order to continue living a conscious existence, you have to transform into a deep and enlightened being? No.

You may make an effort every day to cope with the challenge of continuing to live a conscious life. Having the intention to live a life with greater meaning is the first step towards practising conscious living. When you give more thought to how you conduct your life, you give yourself the gift of more pleasure and contentment.

Taking a Natural and Appropriate Role

Confidence may be gained as well as reflected via self-obligation. People who have a healthy sense of self-confidence believe that they are in control of their own life. They have a sense of organisation and of being adequate to themselves. They accept full responsibility for their feelings, their actions, and their life. It also indicates that you accept responsibility for the outcomes of your choices and behaviours, whether they are good or unpleasant, rather than blaming yourself or others for the consequences of your actions. In order to seek for ways to better and organise things, you need to have the desire to look back and learn from your mistakes.

Young males, in contrast to young women, often exhibit a concentrated and strong nature throughout their adolescent years, which contributes to the development of their independence. At the age of nine, young females' confidence begins to suffer the negative consequences of the situation, and by the time they reach adolescence, they have fallen behind. As one's confidence level drops, feelings of vulnerability and the need for acceptance from others, especially in regard to one's looks, intensify. Although young males are likely to do better on tests than young women, if young women are discouraged from taking risks or pursuing their goals, they may develop a mentality of "I can't" rather than "I can," despite the fact that young men are likely to perform better on tests overall. Such young women may, throughout the course of their lives, develop a distorted mindset about life. This lack of authority and self-assurance has the potential to, in the long run, result in sadness.

Tolerating one's responsibilities in relation to their problems and sadness is necessary to provide the groundwork for structural self-assurance. Then it would be possible to make adjustments to them. An investigation revealed that lottery winners, in the long run, achieved the same exceptional level of affluence as before they won. The pleasure that comes from things like winning the lottery or meeting "Mr. Right" is just fleeting. In the end, our level of happiness is determined by the confidence we have in ourselves as well as the things we think about and do.

What The Opinions Of Other People Are

So, I've shared some of my own experiences with you. However, I am not in isolation, which is why I decided to write this book. This is the reason I not only talk but also mentor and coach. When we help other people, we improve our own well-being and experience a greater sense of fulfilment. I am aware that there are other people who have issues with their self-esteem or confidence, and as a result, I have compiled a list of just some of the struggles with and patterns in self-esteem based on coaching, speaking to people close to me, and research (of course, some of these relate to my own experience as well). I know that there are other people who have issues with their self-esteem or confidence. I haven't written down a tonne of statistics; rather, I've simply jotted down some remarks based on what I've discovered.

On social media, there is a dearth of content geared at building men's self-esteem.

If you look at postings on self-esteem on social media, you will find that women predominate.

It is wonderful that women are more candid about discussing issues related to self-esteem, and if you are a woman who is reading this book to better herself, I want to say thank you. On the other hand, I worry that males would be seen as weak if they reveal their vulnerability, and as a result, it will be repressed. I was afraid about the same thing! I was afraid that if I exhibited vulnerability, a girl wouldn't like me as much, but in reality, now that I show up more as myself, I receive a lot more support from the people who should be supporting me in the first place. It merely means that from time to time, when I have a difficulty or tale to offer, I will share it with you. This does not mean that I will be moaning all the time, since most days I feel fantastic.

It reveals the human aspect of me and the fact that I'm not a robot who smiles all the time.

However, I would want to thank the individuals that do write and share. It's an incredible talent to have. It is perfectly OK if you don't, and I appreciate each and every individual who is reading this; nevertheless, I do hope that by the time you reach the conclusion, I will have helped you become somewhat more open.

There has been an increase in conversation around confidence.

Both self-esteem and confidence may be broken down into its component parts, yet they are inextricably intertwined. Nevertheless, there is more to the concept of confidence. If a person is able to improve their confidence in a skill or area, but they still don't feel wonderful about themselves, then, in my view and based on my own personal experience, it's because their self-esteem has been ignored or they have some work to do in terms of accepting themselves as they are. Just like I had done. I want to talk about having high regard for oneself. Your level of self-esteem affects every aspect of your life, which is why we are going to concentrate on improving it together in this book.

Image of the body

This is not something that I myself have battled with a great deal in the past. Yes, when I was younger I had a few more spots and was a little bit chubbier, but as I got older I managed to get into a decent shape and condition for my age.

Given the relentless pursuit of perfection shown by these models, who are provided with very attractive make-up, lighting, and so on, this is an area that women struggle with. However, males also experience pain. The images of muscle-bound men, men with perfectly chiselled jawlines, and men with flawless skin are not helpful.

I am aware that the height, weight, complexion, and overall appearance of males might make them feel uncomfortable.

Some of these are under our control, while others are not.

I want everyone to feel at ease no matter how they look or act. Despite the fact that I don't have a lot of knowledge in this area, I suddenly recalled something. When I was in my late teens and early twenties, I was obsessed with getting a six pack. I would workout for hours every day. Comparison was a destructive force. When I wasn't doing great, I felt rubbish and continued pushing myself because I didn't like who I saw in the mirror. At times, I did very well, but when I wasn't doing great, I felt rubbish. I wasn't in terrible condition; I simply wasn't 'great' either. By the way, there is no such thing as perfection. Therefore, I shall discuss body image in a later section.

Verification from the outside

This has been the single most destructive force in my life and has done so for a good many years. I am not fully over it, but I am so much stronger than I used to be in my ability to love myself for who I am. People are always searching for validation, whether it comes from their supervisor at work, friends, the person they are dating, family members, or, as is most often the case in today's society, the likes and followers they accumulate on social networking platforms. after I was a small child, I wanted the world around me to be happy, and I wanted my family to be happy after my brother passed away. This desire to make other people happy was the beginning of my people-pleasing behaviour.

In the last ten years, the prevalence of social media has made this problem even worse. Texting and other forms of social media are often used by people as a source of dopamine hits. Action is another topic that is discussed here.

Compared to what

This one is somewhat similar to the last one, but it's not the same. Because of the prevalence of social media and media in general, we are prone to constantly compare ourselves to others. To find out about the most recent author who has released a book that has garnered thousands of followers on social media or on YouTube, all I have to do is search them up. My previous practise consisted of constantly looking at the outcomes and being frustrated that they were not higher, like those of the most successful individuals.

It is beneficial to observe other individuals like Tony Robbins, Gabby Bernstein, and Rob Dial (all of whom are among my faves), but you should never compare yourself to these people since doing so will ruin you.

a state of being alone

It's a terrible feeling to have no one to speak to. It pains my heart that a lot of the postings I read are about how lonely people are. I can almost feel myself as I was when I was a teenager, when I was so lonely yet had no idea how to make friends.

It seems that guys do not want to interact with other people or are unable to do so.

I would want for this to come to an end.

assurance on certain matters

I hear quite a few individuals claim that they struggle with their confidence. It seems that social confidence or dating confidence is becoming more prevalent as a general trend. Permit me to start off by saying that I have been there before with regard to each of these things. To reiterate, confidence is analogous to a muscle; but, in order to exercise confidence, one must first actively take action, and then the emotion will come. Later on in the book, I provide advice on how to improve your self-confidence. My opinion is that having a healthy sense of self-worth will have a beneficial impact on one's confidence.

Step 6 of the Chapter 7 Programme: "Give Up Perfection"

Step 6: Stop Trying to Be Perfect

Perfectionism and low self-esteem go hand in hand with each other. What? What exactly am I referring to? How may perfectionist tendencies go hand in hand with poor self-esteem? Let's take a look at it, along with the reasons why perfectionism causes so many issues.

Is it thus unhealthy to strive for perfection? Is it a terrible thing to want to be the best at what you do and to be the greatest? In reality, perfectionism is a sign of poor self-esteem, anxiety, and uncertainty about one's own abilities. Perfectionism may be harmful, particularly for those who already struggle with poor self-esteem. Therefore, having poor self-esteem may lead to perfectionism, which in turn prevents the individual from embracing themselves as they really are.

People who struggle with poor self-esteem are more likely to be perfectionists because it prevents them from understanding that they are enough just as they are. The pursuit of perfection suggests that who you are is never good enough. Therefore, the conundrum is clear to you.

Problems associated with perfectionism and the factors that contribute to perfectionism

So, what are the consequences of striving for perfection? What are the problematic characteristics of perfectionism, and why is the desire to be perfect considered to be such a negative trait? This is due to the fact that who you are is far more essential than what you do, but the majority of perfectionism focuses on what we do. According to the concept of perfection, we can only be deemed perfect when we carry out our responsibilities without flaw. This is the exact opposite of what you would want someone who struggles with low self-esteem to go through, yet it's exactly what they need.

If you have a poor self-esteem, there is a very likely probability that you also have unreasonable expectations for yourself. The two go hand in hand. Now you just have unrealistic expectations for yourself, and not necessarily for the people around you. The perfectionist is not likely to be content with their physical appearance, their abilities and talents, their accomplishments, or their place in life. Nothing about them will live up to their own standards, and that's frustrating.

This is an argument that goes in circles. Perfectionism may function both as a symptom and a cause of poor self-esteem. It is important to distinguish between the two. The pursuit of perfection necessarily ends in failure because there is no way to achieve it. Giving up the pursuit of perfection will result in an increase in self-esteem and progress towards the realisation that it is sufficient to accept oneself just as one is.

Acknowledge and Celebrate Your Successes

Accepting your accomplishments and celebrating who you are may help you let go of the need to be flawless and enjoy who you are. Do you give yourself credit for your successes, or do you sometimes feel like a fraud because of them? What exactly is the "Imposter Syndrome," though? It is the experience of feeling like a fraud while having a high level of achievement, expertise, and professional standing. Your predisposition towards perfectionism and poor levels of self-esteem prevent you from being able to appreciate the successes you have achieved.

Imposter syndrome is a concept that was established in the 1970s by Dr. Pauline Clance and Dr. SuZanneImes. It refers to a person (often a woman) who is highly competent and efficient but cannot get over their own feelings of inadequacy to obtain a sense of their own authenticity. Imposter syndrome was invented by Dr. Pauline Clance and Dr. SuZanneImes.

Instead of doing this, acknowledge your true accomplishments and take a serious look at the world around you. What is the truth? What exactly is taking place right now? What exactly are the facts surrounding the "situation"?

Accept and Learn from Your Errors

Accepting and learning from your errors is one tried-and-true method for combating low self-esteem. This, along with everything else in this chapter, may seem to be a contradiction, but in reality it is not. Instead of having less self-esteem as a result of your errors, you will discover that you have more of it if you accept responsibility for them and make the effort to learn from them.

The idea that you should take responsibility for your errors is becoming so widely recognised that it is slowly making its way into the culture of many different businesses. Bridgewater, the biggest hedge fund in the world, makes this practise a part of the company's culture. Since it is impossible to achieve perfection, you should accept responsibility for your errors, gain wisdom from them, and even enjoy them.

The Synopsis and the Game Plan

People who struggle with low self-esteem frequently make the mistake of comparing their inner selves with the outside selves of other people, which leads to their perceiving only the negative aspects of themselves. This is due to the fact that what you see from individuals on the exterior is seldom an accurate reflection of who they are on the inside, and it most definitely is not how you perceive yourself.

• Take care of both your body and your mind by giving yourself the attention they need. If you are not performing at your best, you will not be able to accept and learn from the errors you have made, nor will you be able to operate at your best.

- "Decide to Thrive" is the motto you should adopt. After you've finished reading this book by Ariana Huffington, find someone else to talk about it with. Huffington has discovered a strategy that helps her silence the critical voice in her brain so that she may "live a life that matters."

- Give this affirmation a try in order to overcome perfectionism and learn to appreciate everything that you have accomplished. Spread the word widely in all places: 5–10 times per day, you should say, "I embrace my accomplishments!"

The Influence That Optimistic Thinking Can Have

This book explores a simple concept: the transformation of negative thinking into a more optimistic viewpoint. You alone have the power to bring about the desired transformation.

Take control of your own life. Our deeds and responses are entirely the responsibility of each of us. When life hands you lemons, it is not responsible for what you decide to do with them or how you will react to them. You are the only one who can decide whether or not to create lemonade out of those lemons. In the same vein, it is not liable for whether you will feel revitalised or aggravated after you consume it.

You were not unfairly punished by life by having unpleasant experiences befall you. You were dealt a lemon by life in order to offer you an opportunity and a choice. Therefore, you decided to create lemonade out of the situation. I applaud your efforts. You made the conscious decision to seize control of the circumstance and fashion something positive from it. Some individuals opt to focus on the sour aftertaste that is left in their mouths after drinking lemonade and spend the rest of the day bemoaning the unfortunate event that was caused by consuming the beverage. If you do that, you are taking the issue out of your control and allowing life to direct it in a different direction. You choose to point the finger rather than express gratitude. Changing one's point of view is essential if one wants to have a comprehensive understanding of the current predicament. Instead of concentrating on the somewhat unpleasant aftertaste, you should think on the many positive effects that drinking lemonade has on one's health. You forget that drinking may bring you a lot of good in your life if all you do is concentrate on the negative aspects of it. Change your point of view.

Keep in mind that one must have a high level of self-awareness in order to be a master of one's own self. Acquaint yourself with the person who is inside of you. Learn more about that individual. What exactly is it that causes you to start thinking in a negative way? Never dislike someone or pass judgement on them while you piece together the answers. Just make an effort to comprehend that individual.

Recognise the feelings that are now running through your body. Emotion is an essential component of the human experience. We all go through the emotions of anger, worry, fear, sadness, hatred, joy, love, and trust at some point in our lives. Additionally, it might assist us in better comprehending ourselves. In the same proportion as it directs our behaviour, it is also a reflection of who we are as individuals.

The second thing you should do is ask yourself what the rationale is.

Someone once remarked that the reason you dislike someone is because of the mirror that person gives of the aspects of yourself that you dislike. We won't be able to get rid of this feeling until we come to terms with the fact that the person we despise is not to blame for the way we are now feeling. They are not to blame for the pleasure or unhappiness that we experience. To put it another way, the things that other people say and do to us will only have an effect on us if we let them.

Learn to take control of your emotions. It is a force that may either steer us away from something or bring us closer to something. It also helps us distinguish the things that we fear and the things that we want.

Conclusion

I want you to go through the exercises that were developed in this book once again, but this time I want you to dig into more detail since there are a number of reasons why you lack confidence. You need to give yourself more and more reasons to be optimistic as time goes on by engaging in activities that bring you pleasure and gauging your degree of success based on the things you do. Put an end to thinking that your lack of success is because you lack confidence in your abilities. Instead, you should have confidence in the things that you choose to accomplish and acknowledge that other people do not have the same level of confidence in every aspect of their life.

You have to come to terms with the fact that having low self-esteem is the root of the problem. This is based on your life up to this point, but going forward, it should not enter into your life at all. Keep in mind that the opinion of a single individual doesn't really count all that much in the grand scheme of things. I used to believe that it did, and regardless of whether or not I was successful in winning over the favour of my mother, I still went on to do fantastic things, and I continue to do so each and every day of my life without allowing that poor beginning to prevent me from reaching my full potential. You will one day come to the realisation that the way you interpreted anything is not the fault of any negative input, no matter how much of it there was in the world. Who are YOU? Therefore, get rid of any and all of the beliefs that you are insufficient in any form, since the only thing that may make you feel inadequate are thoughts like this. You should strive to be the greatest person that you can be and go through the exercises in this book on a regular basis because each one of them is meant to help you develop confidence and let go of the baggage that you've been carrying around from your past.

Once you are able to accomplish that, you will notice that life is lot simpler for you, and you won't have to spend each day of your life lamenting the person you are because you won't have to change who you are. You are an amazing human being who has a great deal of latent potential. Learn from your mistakes if you end up failing. If you despise your work, you should look for another one. If you despise your life, you have to learn to look at it from a new angle and cultivate both self-confidence and self-esteem at the same time. If you want to change, you have to change. If other people do not treat you with respect, you should not take responsibility for this issue; it is their problem, not yours. If you show respect to the people around you, you will discover that other people are quite responsive to this and that the appropriate sort of people will treat you with the same kind of respect that you show to them. Your life will be much happier once you find that balance in it, and I hope that this book has helped you, even in some tiny way, to reach that point in your life where you can embrace who you are and celebrate it. When you do achieve that balance in life, your life will be a lot happier.

Printed in the USA
CPSIA information can be obtained
at www.ICGtesting.com
LVHW021350051023
760085LV00064B/2007